PAPER BANNERS

▼ ▼ ▼ ▼ ▼

ALSO BY JANE MILLER

PAPER BANNERS

JANE MILLER

Copper Canyon Press

Port Townsend, Washington

Cover art by Colleen Heslin, *Cloudhole,* 2020. Dye on sewn canvas, 244 cm × 302 cm. Courtesy of the artist and Monte Clark Gallery, Vancouver, Canada.

Copper Canyon Press is in residence at Fort Worden State Park in Port Townsend, Washington, under the auspices of Centrum. Centrum is a gathering place for artists and creative thinkers from around the world, students of all ages and backgrounds, and audiences seeking extraordinary cultural enrichment.

LIBRARY OF CONGRESS CATALOGING-IN-PUBLICATION DATA
Names: Miller, Jane, 1949- author.
Title: Paper banners / Jane Miller.
Description: Port Townsend, Washington : Copper Canyon Press, [2023]
Identifiers: LCCN 2023021384 (print) | LCCN 2023021385 (ebook) |
   ISBN 9781556596735 (paperback) | ISBN 9781619322837 (epub)
Subjects: LCGFT: Poetry.
Classification: LCC PS3563.I4116 P36 2023 (print) |
   LCC PS3563.I4116 (ebook) | DDC 811/.54—dc23/eng/20230508
LC record available at https://lccn.loc.gov/2023021384
LC ebook record available at https://lccn.loc.gov/2023021385

COPPER CANYON PRESS
Post Office Box 271
Port Townsend, Washington 98368
www.coppercanyonpress.org

for Valyntina

CONTENTS

III

PAPER BANNERS
▼ ▼ ▼ ▼ ▼

THE GRAND PIANO

Our five thousand years are up.
We are going to die violently.
The housekeepers and gardeners burn the furniture
outside the palace in golden light.
The beekeepers weep over the last red milkweeds.
The artists remove the scaffolding.
Our job is brutal and necessary:
to be with the one we love and to think
something in the heart weighs on the heart.

THE LOVERS

Don't misunderstand me, beloved.
Were I to climb toward the moon,
I could consume a flask of fine wine

before coming down Mount Tai
among schoolchildren, elderly, and pilgrims.
My legs, back, heart, all good, my beloved.

One hikes the stone steps in the dark
to see the sunrise from the peak,
the Yellow Sea stained by sands of the Gobi.

And yet, now that I have reached
the age you were when you died,
the Temple of Azure Clouds has transformed

into bamboo, paper, and satin, a fan
that is closed to me. On the night trek
one would miss the sultry pink

petals of peach trees blossoming.
You whom I have never seen,
who cannot keep the petals from falling,

how you endured
the loss of your husband
until he became a stick of incense

is beyond me.
The melon cart has turned over.
I've lost my property and my ax.

I beg you, please come to me.
I despair that you will not.
I was born a seabird

who flew from wet weeds into darkness
to alight on a stone pillow.
It would be a great pity

if time was our real barricade.
I have poured jasmine with lemon
and mountain honey, and being alive,

I intend to drink it. It is the green Lorca
drank, and how he survives on magpies.
Autumn colors will follow,

a festival of horses in a stream of agony.
Poetry does not need to give birth to a prince,
nor must anyone understand.

It will go on in the army camps,
in the jade towers, in the bitter bureaucracies
of eternity. It will fall from the widow's hairpins.

HARMLESS ODE WITH OSIP MANDELSTAM

When you are young you think everything
depends on the results
of one night

you bicycle home
late
in a white shirt

the air throws back
a song you're singing
no one is around

no someone's dog
is crying
following you

the cape curves
along a salty bay
gently

you follow the arc
of a good idea
with no horizon

in the off-season
the water appears
to have risen

a woman
made you feel
the immense

breathing far inside
a foghorn
every so often

when she came
you would pour her
liquid she would comb

you with long hair
you wheel so slowly
to stay the feeling

for the artist
there is the story
you are writing

and the story of writing it
when older
neither matters

the shooting stars
the silver bicycle
the shirt the streetlamps

forget as you forget
the desire that made you
dress and depart mysteriously

your spirit
travels inward
time

is someone
with a hand down your throat
trying to dig out

what you sound like
alone
elusive as blue malva

sprinkled
over her bell
to arouse her

planted
on the grave
of the ancients

the dead feed
on the aphrodisiac
to return to form

its flower and leaf
salve each wound
of the nether world

the viscous heart
of the root
is a throat

emollient
to comfort the windpipe
on its journey from the lungs

listen
I have no manuscripts
Mandelstam said

no notebooks no archives
I alone in Russia work
from the voice

the artist frees
but a few words
like figures from steam

as pain clouds experience
to make plain
all is empty

all is luminous
the gears of illness
still

the wheels of drama
pause on the road planks
for you to fathom

the clear night
deep inside
as a Tang poet wrote

splatters of sudden rain
like pearls large and small
on a jade plate

JADE RIVER

I can walk to it from this rented house.
I have swum across it.
Anyone can borrow a boat and fish there.
Just today, a pudgy old man fell in.
Broke the surface with his backside, trolling for carp.
A bare ass like a bald head
disappeared out of its floating shorts.
His rolling belly below a shrunk shirt,
how cool it must have felt,
after the shock. Nearly naked like Buddha and absent awhile.
He surfaced and did not look around,
except for his skiff. Still there,
lucky for him. He spoke to himself
while he rubbed his face like a little boy.
From this I infer everything about life
because of course
life is a simple matter of failure.
Simply part of a flow,
I know now. Until it happens to me.
Then I forget, thinking it important.
Attracted by a fleeting glance of a fairy
in a chandelier the size of France,
no, of China, one is not really sure
existed. But for a minute.
Then I am bereft again.
As to the river, I understand
jade is a famous feng shui mineral.

Confucius wrote that it is like virtue
and its brightness represents heaven.
The healing power of a flower
is a dream of the gentle stone.
You see the mass-produced gem shaped
into turtles, dragons and fish too,
in your home country.
Because you are loud and young
in a lithe body with a splashing energy
of a puppy, a stray,
I never thought I could love you.
I sought peace at seventy.
A jade river inside me. Green. Slow.
Long life, I said to friends,
and inside said, Poetry, over.
Money, spent. Parents, buried. Brother,
lost. Childless. And my beloved disappears
inventing day and night in her studio.
As busy as a bee, as the fake poets used to say.
Now they say, busy as a walrus hanging
upside down in the stately tree of death, to be creative
and funny, because of the tragic world.
Must you stand on a bare branch, and why
should I care? What if I cry
when I greet you? None of it matters
a hoot, as is said in imitation
of the great owl, rarely seen,
but more important than ever.
More important, rarely seen, great owl,

some things I would never say
before, because they sound
imitative, common. Except now
I get perfectly what is "important."
What is "bare" and "more."
One never knows which words
get one imprisoned
tortured and murdered
so every one is exemplary
and depends on whoever
designates their meaning.
The words skinned alive.
The words sexual freedom.
It's the same in America and China,
the world over. I wake
with a dread of you in a jail
for ten subversions or a hundred
against an emperor or mother.
I blow by every somnambulist
in the dream and fly to you.
Why can't you simply
fear and admire,
rather than wander as smoke,
smoking, rolling bourbon around
your mouth, sucking men's nipples
and more in the ether streets
of your country, only recently a child.
As Rimbaud would say, so much the worse
for the wood that discovers it's a violin.

One of your many instruments,
no doubt, another gift I don't know about.
If your poems survive the age,
if the earth survives us,
may mercy find you
in the mouth of a river
in the lap of an emperor
made of palladium leaf,
steel pins, walnut ink,
and thousands of green glass marbles.
You were born to mutilate the old rules.
The rest is heroic and belongs to you.

IDYLL

As the immortals used to ride on huge lotus flowers
the mind ferries a spirit on its bamboo mat
carried as a refugee carries water
in a bucket on her head

until its bottom breaks through
in a moment of bliss a few precious mementos
one's smile one's youth
pass nimbly through the universe

it is true our people left behind fields of hemp and citrus
threaded with gold
their sweat fell as rain
until a different season brought a chill

time has chiseled titles and praises
but we are not included
even if heaven is deep blue and endless
it cannot explain our wild love

saved in an alphabet of moss
the past cannot engrave its virtues
they remain as our ancestors
buried with the days

I am embarrassed to go out
among so many in a hurry
I trim the lamp's smoking wick
I take off my clothes

the fumes of wine and blossoms
are by nature fleeting
in cold weather they lose their fragrance
although I have studied poems I only now notice

they are not about farewell
in exchange for giving up land
the refugees sought a boat and a tent
but only received a decree

it is still a perilous time
the wealthy will regret it
although my flute is quiet
my senses have not deteriorated

yes I've been too lazy to wash my hair
or stamp my papers as the situation permits
apprentices may ask about a spirit
perfumed as incense or steeping tea

just shy of life
you will be alive again in a shape
of fruitful meditation
like a beloved fig tree that follows you into exile

as if I had from time to time
eaten a sacred mushroom
even if your boat returns empty because of a storm
I have to acknowledge it

the beauty of form

AESTHETIC ARGUMENT

Thrashers pierce pomegranates.
They hurt the quiet.
Who can blame them?

Only an owl will deter them.
But owls are rare.
There's no metaphor here.

I want the red fruit.
I would share it,
if their beaks didn't open

each one. Don't think me unlucky.
I have been a servant of love,
I don't care what they say

about love spoiling like fruit.
Even grief
should not be wasted.

The scarlet blooms
will not return anytime soon.
I want to

see them next spring,
not be under a blanket of frost.
I'm tired,

wrapping cloth around,
stepping out of a cold bath,
standing in a doorway.

A neighbor drags her collie through the night.
A sweetness of pine,
citrus, and rosemary

clings to my heart
from the old world. Remember?
The myth of someone

to dissolve
the laws governing matter,
its wild branches scratching

kingfisher green and white
details on a handscroll.
Friends, better to forgive yourself

in order to write.
I draw the shade.
A dry odor

plays over a sheet of paper.
An envoy carries a tray
of fresh radiance.

We are doomed to part
in an orchard of apricots
ten thousand miles away.

THE THATCHED COTTAGE

Before the rain, high winds sweep
three layers of thatch off the poet's roof.
Straw flies over the creek,

scatters into the treetops or a ditch.
I feel that I'm barely holding up
a candle in the night in Du Fu's poem

when reeds blow from the pitch,
leaving his children rained on in their beds.
In the end we grant how impossibly fragile

his dream would have been
of a mansion with ten thousand rooms
for our worldly scholars and our poor.

We older poets remember him
trying slowly to go home,
floating down the Yangtze

but not getting there, not quite.
Yellow orchids climb the trellis
of his cottage, really a hut,

while catfish chase the rushes.
The old man's out front now
in bronze,

far from your white marble *David*,
straggly-bearded, modest in size,
nothing like the towering nude

in full flower in a gilded hall.
Hell, no,
just an old fool outside in a tunic

with a walking stick.
Might Michelangelo whittle
his immortal Tuscan into snow

in trade for one more
herbaceous meal with mead
and a young poet on his lap.

Maybe an iris or a crocus
is something splashed in sun
you will live to see, my friend,

almost an unreal shade
of beauty in a bare vineyard.
Were we really here to feel

god's mangy fingers
poke our mortal body
like raw meat

into a riddled honeycomb
of art? After it rains hard enough,
the grasses rot. One spring

I met a young poet of Chengdu
by Flower Rinsing Creek,
studying the rain glitter

on rushes and straw that once
covered the famous site,
as clear-cut words

cover plain paper,
poorly, if necessarily. I am sorry
but I don't know why,

after everything you've given
and forgiven in this realm,
it withers your torn root

and clangs a stray howl
of fate cold as iron.
Should a lamb not have given its wool?

THE MISSING APRICOT TREE

Long ago, when we met, and had to
separate, you sent a picture
of you squatting by a river,
bathing, your face half-turned, looking
over your shoulder beyond me
into a monastery, and beyond that,
daughters hanging threadbare laundry.
We were ourselves
so young. I longed for your return,
and in springtime, although the wildflowers
were few, we lived together.
Hundreds of fireflies
accompanied us in dream,
swarming in the birches
out the uncurtained windows.
They alarmed us, and the cries of returning geese
drove us farther under the covers.
We never stopped talking of their beauty,
although the years parted us forever.
In the full moon's light
on an empty bed,
the white geese and firefly glow
dissolve. We vanished as gently

as snowfall on a face.
I forgot to give you a parting gift.
Then silence. Not to be confused with emotion.
Anise rises from the village.
And a missing apricot tree
becomes as massive as the past.
The five white petals of its blossom
survive as I do,
as spring energy
in an aging body.
Another night of a big moon.
I roll in and out of its light, wondering,
late autumn, how is it
that I could lose my first love
as carelessly as a line of verse
that made the whole work.
Not that art perishes.
Nor is love
only about pleasure.
I still need to thank
the old gods in the rocky earth
for all that has happened.
This stick will have to be a tree.

ENFLAMED ODE

In the parlors of history
the swish of silk a clasped hand
at a private party
embers of a late hour
not where I would've trespassed

in a strapless gown
or groom's suit
nor leapt from a horse
with a molten invitation
to the foot of a bed

my soul has confessed
with paper and pencil
not what I would have said
if I had thought about it
or read more or traveled

and yet I have never wanted to
return alone nor have left
without offering something at least
best knit on a pillow cover
or printed on a chopstick

untutored sleuths
as you have found me forgive me
I've broached the subject of love
incautiously without success
without desire after a while

I have wanted only for you
to feel free and live fully
a double happiness
bold as a bobcat in the open
while I have hardly finished a quintet

good enough to paint above a door
or on a child's headboard
I've done nothing purely
to deserve this desert or heat
where the perfect end would be

could I but offer water

◀ II ▶

PAPER BANNERS

The ancients claim
that lightning
pierces the agave,
cooking its heart
to release an elixir.
Smoke in a doorway.
A wren *chirr*s.
An old adobe returns
to mud and dung.
Fools dream of crossing
the desert in a boat
with its banner to the future.
Pain remembers pain
and death pisses
into a firepit.
That leaves today
a tumbleweed of hot wind.
More praise
goes to soldiers
than to poets
asleep somewhere cool.
Snapped to
as if struck
by a drunken car
to praise the wren,
the wolf, the open.
Maybe forgive them
hanging around
the mezcal
foretelling events
once fired in earth.
Mashed and fermented,

rank of grilled corn
and singed fruit.

Life's no rat
in a raincoat.
Poor being will thrash
getting out
of Jane's skeleton.
Hope violets grow
heart-shaped dark
green leaves in her loam.
The past? Bulldozed
as the light
comes back up
tomorrow.
I live to tell it.
But one strophe
of Sappho's
scarlet feelings
(*all is to be dared . . .*)
pulped the safe pages
I wrote. Given your life
is smoke in a doorway,
what can you say?
Pain begets pain
and death starves
its own wound.
Come dawn the sky
shimmers of emeralds,
green wine bottles
empty, stacked on a table.
They say the cosmos
isn't hostile.
Yet strangles a dove
with one hand.

AUGURY

The night's headlamps
took off hours ago
through the mesquites,
toward the south, to light
a slim figure over the border
wall. A high wail
keeps traveling north
when she gets stopped.
It rips through
our middle-class bullshit.
It wonders if we care
no more than another
neighbor dog cowering.

A flamboyant plant
disrobes in a gust.
We listen to Nina Simone
spit fire. Burn a piano.
The wind fights back.
We see the flames in her eyes.
Every woman's form
of protest varies,
not in nature but in scale.
Because I am not myself
alone, now must atone
for the woman retching
in detention, spared the illusion

of suffering because it's real.
Another hot summer
wanders without drinking water.
Love breaks in as if it's her old

apartment, lies on your coverlet.
A fool with a decaled knapsack
on the precipice of the unknown.
Asks for a thunderstorm
then crosses the wash.
Forgives us our privilege,
making pizza in Blast Oven,
Arizona. Burnt on the rack
by the rising sun,

a throbbing heart.
Her sobbing keens
over the suburbs. Am I
to believe love, not war,
a solution? I try to
hold a long time,
but time refuses. Asks us
what part of the regime
are we? A tongue of hot road
slips into the backyard.
Safe, spent.
Our melodrama protected
by a tin fence.

AT THE MAGISTRATE

Chuff chuff chuff of helicopters. Whinny of frightened horses. *¡Ay! ¡Ay!* children call and cry. In a distant country, their parents live off goats and boats. Some ignoble order from a white world has locked brown children in cages. Their hopes kindle like newspaper and extinguish quickly. Before disappearing, some are carried on a distant train of bones or an angry river.

Down the hall there's a wedding. It's normal. The children resemble their guards. The guards could be their older brothers ignoring them, talking crap about girls or cars. A form of honesty, of aging. The agony is they're torn apart like strips of Angus beef hoisted onto a roof, a local favorite, lime-marinated and dried in cages a good twenty-four hours on a rack in the sun,

served pan-fried to deputized ranchers sporting badges outside the magistrate. Used to shouting at cattle, one barks at the wife on his cell. One parks a warm pistol on a table. The patio attracts the poor who live outdoors and those who police them. Some are stripped down to shorts and straw hats, but the marshals are branded into their outfits, *sweating bullets,*

one blurts. They bother to lean over their potbellies to urinate in ninety degrees. Squeeze themselves around a plastic tablecloth decorated with tequila shots. An hour here is a long time in the sun. They twist on metal stools, a few spit-roasted goats dripping from the heat. Toddlers play with water guns. Vultures feed on mice. Everybody's hungry one way or the other. The one with the razor-sharp uniform,

the youngest, muses, *I remember my grandmother half-dead,* he says, *from plucking hens,* feeding him ices all summer after her stroke, fingers curled into a little fist. *Mi pugilista pequeña,* his grandfather would call her, although he tried to kill her over liquor. The gun on the table quivers as a helicopter lowers another tender-aged inmate over the downtown. *Los sheriffs* joke about what it meant to be kids, to be free. *I stuck my head in a freezer once,* the bald guy crows, *one August, and burned an ear.* Then he stands up to exhibit the scar, proudly, a teenager again, before turning inside to command his young guns, *vengan aquí,* go, stay, come, like dogs he raised. Six months ago they were in high school, now they loiter in body armor, casually passing themselves a canteen of water around

the courthouse, asking what to do. *Take this cup from me,* Vallejo said famously, *aparta de mí este cáliz,* in a mere sheaf of fifteen poems, each facing the other: *Do not die; I love you so!* With their water gone, the patrol moves on. Nobody's told them Coke is dehydrating. They're hanging by the vending machines when a guard bets, *I'm either them—* pointing to the cages—*or him*—they can smell the tequila coming

toward them—tightening his gun strap, says, *I hate him.* The concrete courthouse settles another inch. Its architect placed the windows to center the mountains. The children climb them trying to escape. Researchers dress pig carcasses in sneakers, pants, and shirts to study migrants who perish in the desert. It's normal. *¡Ay!* squeals a chunk of pink tenderloin curled like a baby on its side.

Everyone needs the sun to set quickly.

HOMAGE TO ORDER WITH DISORDER
IN LAST STANZA

The fire station's aluminum siding
plummets with a clang

splashed in noise is a message
to feel how you feel

if you ran over your dog
and wanted to open your wrist

and howl to yourself
knowing the self is a poor shell

with which to hear the universe
one of its most expressive markings

is to play a piece so it sounds
like a nightingale with a toothache

explaining the nature of reality
repulses tradition

the music seems to accompany an ancient ritual
akin to the gods clearing the street

with unholy heat
tourists should not need to carry

loaded guns to break the fearsome
silence without

a summer of modest proportions
girls skipping in dotted sundresses

the town's matriarchs
bent in shawls

leaving church again accepting a god
made clean washed by his blood

I cannot abide piety yet
passion I greatly admire

in a million towns like this
death hides its hemorrhaging belly

in shadows of a sunny afternoon
you hear the summons

of an internal structure
as a piece of music

out of earshot
free as a creek

over rocks
absent humanity's clack

could you learn to feel more
connected in a desert

if everything suddenly emptied
could you hold that snake

lose yourself
in the composition

drive the streets of Tucson
see not a single person

awaiting a bus
or crossing to the library in the sun

forget me
searching for my car

on a garage roof
looking downwind for a monsoon

nobody clicked into handcuffs
or chugging beers on a cement terrace

the churro shop
boarded up

no more dough piped
from a star-tipped pastry bag

no lonesome dog

CHEKHOV PARKS HIS CORVETTE

Sex worker arrests convulse again.
She loses good jewelry and makeup
getting away. But they get her
sister. On the face of things,
a clenched jaw. Dogs yelping to sirens.
Guns, candlelight. A motorcycle

saws through masked students.
Somebody sings, strong, not pure.
Irony can't cut it.
Surrealism, I forgive you too.
You haven't gone far enough.
You can't get the guts

spilled in the street
back into the body,
but prefer to serve it
as sheep intestines
for fine dining on Mars.
You've gone too far

from what the mind is for
after the problem of war
changes to hunger
and hunger murders
one's brother.
The woman whose body

spends the weekend
in jail standing, lost
those nights like so many others
god tortured
into human form. You're pretty
stoned. That is a lot of smoke

up your false chimney
in the shape of a rocket, falling back
with its capsized canoe of mathematicians,
as you put it to us. Amusing,
until they walk over
to the strip club, shrinking

when they're slapped
or dying of a stroke
solemnly on sateen sheets.
Others wait like lovebirds on a fence
to fuck in ten seconds.
The humidity counts to a hundred.

The days of the week bleed out
into the street. Shots crack. Words fire
at one another. The truth is going to
expose you in your belled hat
and pointy shoes, entertaining
as someone's pet. Walk your cat

around the block, presto,
you're home again and nobody
notices. Just don't be pissing
on your curled toes in the yard
when an imagined civil guard
asks for your documents.

Concerned by a fillip
he has read, Anton Chekhov
arrives and parks his Corvette.
He can't stand it,
a gift from the American
cooking him dinner

in a fictitious kitchen.
He reminds himself of a patient

with heart palpitations
lined up to see him
in their village of Melikhovo
who has little hope of a cure.

Death drives that carriage
out of control down cobblestones.
The doctor stoops to baby a mutt
with a look of helpless anger
at the golden vegetables
that made it sick.

He suspects a scoundrel
sprinkled anise seeds, an aphrodisiac
abused by the same ilk
who trashes a woman for being
shameless about stretch marks.
As the peasants say of the sort

who won't pay her
in a story by the good Russian,
he has risen so high in the world
that he is quite out of reach now.
You must walk into the countryside
to smell the steaming dung and new milk.

BIRD WITH ONE LEG

Thank you for learning English
and pausing to read this.
Thanks, too, for what must have been
very long hours on a plane
alone, thirsty, not in first class,
when you traveled to this place
to study
what, poetry?

What were you thinking,
I wonder, pretending
to be manly, worldly,
although you had a high degree,
once respected here, of learning.
And a history, already, of books,
with a rather strange look of bliss
under that shock of black hair.

Perhaps your mother made you
get a haircut for the trip, or new
shoes, or better glasses.
Your welcome must have been quiet,
I imagine in the middle of a night.
Or not, maybe a lively morning
in an airport near a cornfield.
Possibly met with a frown

from a dull uncle or sad friend.
The truth is I know little
of your circumstance or habits.
I almost hear your funny laugh
entertaining the busy bus driver,
hoping to cover a bit of fear
with perfect English
in search of the Wild West

you read about. What's left
for a thoroughbred
if this country is bridled
by steely-haired white men.
Nevertheless, or because,
thank you for persevering
in our poor language of similes,
adjectives, and multisyllables.

It is a young alphabet
not worthy of a performance
such as yours, deft with craft
like a flamethrower's or juggler's.
Well, the world will sip
from a substantially different cocktail
and wake drunk and stay young
the more you write about it.

Also, I'm pretty sure as a poet
with a sense of wit
and a tragic vision, you'll find
yourself a serious lover. God
help English then, when you rip it up
and rewrite that hetero Ovid!
Thank you for journeying from the East
for our chance meeting,

crazy as a bank heist in Texas
with pop guns and sparklers.
A child bubbling furiously
as hot red chile oil spiked
in native citrus-scented
peppercorns and hot black vinegar,
raised on fermented bean paste,
cold sliced beef, cold diced rabbit,

what would he want
with ketchup-painted fries?
I apologize.
May you follow your tea leaves
and stars, and not the false gods
who left a good boy
motherless many ages ago
in a pear tree, watching

deliveries enter Venice, slowly
learning the Chinese on their boxes.
O the sorrowful Marco Polo,
not ten thousand horsemen
guarding an emperor
fanned with cobalt feathers,
nor a pleasure dome of gilded cane
in a land famed for bridges and prostitutes,

not even a dulcimer-playing maiden
singing of a holy mountain
softens that child's memory
when his merchant father
takes Marco for twenty-five years
into the vast Asian lands,
from which blossoms
a *Book of the World's Marvels.*

What is the innocence
or experience upon
which your greatness depends,
my friend, the pink blush
of white blossoms, fallen snow,
a drowning leaf?
The Italian wrote of a magician
levitating golden cups

in a palace braced by silk cords,
and a sorcerer turning a dead body
into gold easily as an emperor
into an elephant. Fantasy
for a poet may be a thought
awake, whistling
far from its meaning.
(On a birthday spent away,

are you ok?) Twenty-five years!
In the strange place of one's own
skin as a portal for storms.
At your age, Confucius met a bird
on one leg predicting rain,
and folly for those
who dug no drain.
Better prepare a deep pool

of patience to weather
empty vessel, flooded vessel.
As you feel the chill
of history coming on,
you must manage
to be borne
hurtling from family
toward eternity.

POMPEII

Prefers the couch for a nap
poor self ultimately neurotic and romantic
actually has lice
snowboard on acid and you hit Sophocles

HAVE COURAGE AND BE KIND

They scout to see if I am worthy
of their whole colony.
Paper wasps, so called for
chewed plant stems and dead wood
in their comb. Noble building!

Legend avers that Lao Tzu was born
an old man with long earlobes.
Or conceived when his mother saw
a falling star. To the mind that is still,
he teaches,

the whole universe surrenders.
I should leave the bobcat
splayed under a fig tree,
casual as a coat flung at a party,
well enough alone,

as mother advised about poetry.
I also have not served honorably
the arm's-length rattlesnake
ringed around a date palm.
Mind like a mad monkey

isn't attractive or funny. The sages argue
the vinegar is sour,
bitter, or sweet,
depending on their worldview,
and if the world is full of suffering,

it is for something.
But I have only now
put my feet up to contemplate. Help.
Scholar of sojourns,
where are the days

without complaint? Where the oasis?
Trembling and rage
nest in my head and no one
to sort, swat, or train them.
A rash action

may cause the ruin
of the most important
female in the village,
the healer. It's personal,
swimming with wasps,

as the saguaro implies
growing slowly every century.
Inside the green gate
of the lagoon,
learning not to drown

the hero that stings me.

MEADOW WITH STANDING CROWS

After living in the sprouting desert there is nothing
I'd prefer more than the thought
of sweet rain falling into a salty bay.
Rather than bare the farthest touch,
rather than be rain, having been
neither of this world nor mad as it turns
out, on and off during a year
I saw someone had bitten your neck near the baby
hair, and also your shoulder. Why does it show,
is it of the heart, is it mindless, jealousy,
where nothing moves in a field in a world, and it is morning?
Even though you never came after me
all summer, nor called, not once
when I said not to, like finally
stepping over water after contemplation of it
as sand, two crows in the moans of the shallows
in my head answer for whom are we mysterious
and suffering, for loveliness.

JASMINE IN A FOREIGN COUNTRY

starts in a car with a flat tire
I wouldn't stop to change
you thought better
to plug and inflate it
than miss our destination altogether
then you touched me in the sea air gently
as the princess under whose mattress lay the pea
as a reminder of the majesty of a gesture
it had been so long it felt like
a fork stuck into a potato
tonight I thought that if for some tectonic reason
you left this galaxy first
I would rather flee the house
into shark waters or be imprisoned
in a superstore with a sniper
than hurry my next reality one jot
that jot is how I appear
in a terribly expanding universe whose
tilted martini above the craven tavern
pours down a noble glass of neon
such as spills out my heart
inside a fight to the finish fizzles
while outside the lone station
the gas line catches fire with bare hands
squeezing the wheel of a wheezing automobile
I go bizarrely slowly
so nowhere
to pull up fill up or repair
if anyone could please leave my self by the side of the road
in good time it would smell sweet

FUNDAMENTALS

FRESHLY SEEDED GRASS

When artists emerge from a society
which could collapse by sunset,
they stop by a pavilion where ale is made.
Let joy be joy, one opines.

Just as the sweet infusion of wort
contacts the yeast mash,
the nudes on their canvases
sprout goosebumps.

LEMON CUSTARD

What will survive of us is love,
the oldest provision known
as disarmingly sweet and tart.

SQUASHED FROG

A lover's quarrel is like a launch into a cobweb.

In the dark I pee beside a prickly pear,
nearly poke my personals
meditating on desire.

Unfortunately it is sex
which kills the spider under the spider.

MY MOTHER'S POSTCARDS

In the darkroom of my teens,
she wrests back my frizzy hair into a tight pony.

Not even an army could control
my agony as the picture snapped.

I appear as her victim,
but the heat from my scalp
sears her Anthropocene hands.

Yeah, it's a dogfight,
one of many images
of reprimand.

WESTERN PHILOSOPHY

The great thinker preferred
to toss jacks into the air
on the steps of the Temple of Artemis
rather than execute laws.

If character is destiny,
as Heraclitus claimed,
stepping into a river,

slipping, wading, or swimming,
it's always the same, always something,
too cold, quick current, low branches, whatever.

As the river shifts, is it still
the same river? I can't make up my mind.
The metaphysics is fishy
and has made me sad.

Nature endures by changing
and dispersing. The thought
calms my nerves, but afternoon
vanishes, and I can't
find my murky way out.

Moonlight or lightning enters from long ago
or tomorrow, this autumn or the next.
(The poem can't make up its mind.)
I crawl home,

settled for the time being
as an owl on a pole or an egg on a plate.

Bunnies, those poor suckers,
stuck on ice in the flowing river,
squeal like babies on an airplane.

CRYING WITH JONI MITCHELL
IN MY HEADPHONES ON A PLANE

Even if all the apples leap from their crates at a market,
poetry has less hysterical energy than dating.

TEMPTATION OF CHRIST

A warm day in February surprises everybody,

but by dusk's enchanting light
the lemons freeze on the tree.

Language has its reality also.
It understands bastardized pain

but it can never feel like a cut artery.

PRACTICE AFTER CLASS

An anecdote about early Dutch artists
is like a tree in a sieve.

It makes no sense
in broad daylight
because they loved muted colors.

When children paint the tree,
perhaps they would welcome it
if you play the flute at twilight.

SENTIMENTAL SONG

No rain but the south portico of the Forum is dripping.

PLAN AND CROSS-SECTION

Switch on an iron chandelier.

See a blind woman finishing a portrait.

Carve a large portal into the house.

Enjoy slow sex facing a blue wall.

PATHETIC FALLACY

When clouds are sullen
they moan into their soft pillows.

Like a cloud, the self is a construct.
It leads to craving that leads to crying.

We wander the villages and forests
of suffering and happiness.

Hush! If you pay attention,

rain and kindness are identical.
They clear your mind.

SAY NOTHING MAKE NO INTERPRETATIONS

To dive for oysters for the pearl
begs the question
whether I deserve it
or a jellyfish sting.

POPPING BUBBLY IN AN EMERGENCY

We plant green tomatoes in a monsoon.
Before they appear she will paint them.

I HEAR SINGING FROM A BAGUETTE

You're floating naked
wearing sunglasses in a pool.

It's like when Monroe answers *perfume*
for what she wears to bed.

The problem is there's no bottom
to sexism and stardom.

BREAD PEEL WITH TWELVE-INCH HANDLE

The map is out of all proportion to the motherland,
but the beans smell of onions cooked over wood.

FUNNY I WAS JUST THINKING ABOUT YOU

Milk and eggs fill the shelves
a while longer.
The taverns never emptied.

We didn't understand the war
would resume that didn't let us
hold hands, wouldn't let us
rent a room with one bed.
Those were their weapons.

Before it gets worse
tomorrow, or Tuesday,
with a mass shooting
or a dress stripped off a man,
what was it you said to me
about your country,

that there was no word for privacy?
And that's how it starts again here,
a word disappears.

ELEGY WITH LAST LINE PLAYED ON A PIANO

I lost you easily as music from a passing car.
Sometimes I wonder whether you are driving it
or you are dead.
O pure fragrance . . .

THE BABY JESUS

We roll up the pastel rug
that once lay in a horse stall,

crumble the *Arizona Daily Star*
to clean our sun-fired tiles.

On all fours,
scrub with water, white vinegar,
and baking soda.

Later, Valyntina sips tequila.

What will survive of us is love,
not the marble floors of the Vatican.

SOUTHERN LINE BOXCAR GRAFFITI

On the way to see Van Gogh's *Almond Blossom,*
we learn he left it to his nephew

named after him. The snowy flowers
represented hope to Vincent.

Spray-painted on the outside of our train,
"O honey meet me at the end of the world."

SUNSHOWER

Think about how much pleasure
can be morally ambiguous,

visibly glistening on the rack
fresh from the abattoir, for example,
the softest, reddest leather boots.

What about ten centuries, maybe twenty,
of walled towns over ancient cisterns

built by slaves, and more life
in the museums, churches, and frescoes
made by artists working for gruel?

Outdoors an immigrant wipes down a table
so the parliamentarian can blow his nose in peace.

A nurse sits on a newspaper on a break with a coffee.
The priest's poodle eats dried figs
before wetting my leg.

All this Western culture for no good reason
crystallized around noon.

By now I should explain
at seventy what was happening at twenty
when a freckly, poorly slept, unwashed volunteer

wrote, "I'm lonely, god help me, lonely as a . . ."
and couldn't say into her spiral notebook,

nor earn a morsel of a young calf's pounded meat
served to her with grated lemon and green oil,
such as Caravaggio was rumored to eat

after killing a man plucking whores from the piazza.
Because the artist must compete for models,

he sets out with a dirty sword
to make mincemeat of his enemy's testicles,
but mistakes the femoral artery for the groin,

such that a pimp like himself bleeds to death in the street.
Apparently art separates man from beast only so far,

as surprising as a sunny day
with sudden rain on knit baby clothes
by a table of ladies' old-world

chiffon, fine as new. A musician frail as dew
wears his guitar under his poncho.

Are these passing droplets beautiful
or the nubilous spit of another
of my false starts as purveyor of illusions

solid as a big table with hard cheeses,
unleavened bread and barrel wine at the ready?

For the sufferer in the agora
without an elegant solution,
let it be spun of airy old gold

when the tarpaulin is pulled back
on the catfish with moist eyes.

CHILDREN VERSUS GENERALS

The bullet train stops to get the freshest meat from the vendors
it carries a returning army and the grown children are hungry

they wave shirts out the windows
the hero is hungover and refuses to be photographed

history knows his face anyway he's eighteen
his gelled hair is roughed-up and his beard's a month old

he's so pretty he could be in a war movie
if I stop now and write not a single word

will you get him a cool washcloth
be him or ignore him

remember I need you to finish this
without you I am as lonely as a split melon

covered in flies at a station stop
or saturated in lead paint in Renaissance art

what is this poem compared to
one of Caravaggio's blackened torches

whose embers start a war
an exaggeration forgive me I am

but a poor student of art
boarding to visit my dead mother

◄ III ►

ELEGY WITH LAST LINES IN THE FORM OF HAIKU

She died one winter evening.
As through a window of a poem
a princess escapes.

She saw it not as a process
but as a flaw. Perhaps control
served a form of love,

of faithfulness.
Of mother slipping behind,
It's a form of madness,

said the doctor, as the poets say
the moon slips behind a cloud.
The end state of a tidal pull.

Or as the mystics prefer, *absent,*
or, as mother seems to be,
omnipresent

since we buried her,
and by *we,* I mean,
light, dark, mystery, fertility, and time.

Moonbeam on the bay,
she slips silently into
a satin nightgown.

THE PLOT OF *HAMLET*

Given the mother of anger is physical
when I hurt she put my mattress near hers

crimping a starched sheet into peaks
she'd roll marbles down our bent knees

imploring the wheels of our chariots
to speed down the mountain of history

she was a nervous rider
not meaning to beat the horses

other than that we fought
to outsmart childhood and adolescence

failing this failing that
one day I tell myself *you were unconscious*

if we think about life in earlier times
day follows night the rest is gossip

THE CALL TO MINDFULNESS

sounds like dawn at the boat basin,
saffron-robed monks ringing bowls laughing

where there might have been tears
when they found out that you stole their mallets.

The burden is on you, prince, in pursuit of your ruin,
and me for not flushing you out like a duck in the wetlands.

I couldn't not know they shot them there
along the shoreline of the shallows

of the once vaunted palisade. In their royal robes,
the dead deserve an explanation as to where they've gone.

It's our time, we should get ready,
and absolutely no living backwards. No resuscitating.

The lit bridge is flashing. Only a last toll to pay
if we're going to take that lonesome drive

around the leveled cliffs in your sky-blue convertible
up the hill toward the high school.

Slow down and let me out now.
There's a girl I loved, she's probably dead.

Is fate set into a network of felicitous meetings?
Should I plan on losing you again?

O are you home or being tamed by the river?
It's our time, we should get ready.

The bridge's necklace winks so pretty.
Late to get on our knees

to slide the family ranch house into the flotsam.
Floating away beyond reach,

that's a sick smell
of liver from the meat grinder.

It's time to go into the city.
With your hand out in greeting,

you might be returning
the spoils. A moment of cheer

I mistake for charity. My brother,
isn't our nightmare sheer as an orchid

exposed to the sun for reasons that, in pursuit
of our ruin, the imagination strains after,

bent scribbling on the steely surface of purple night.

ROADHOUSE

You could hear a hairpin hit the straw
until the sun shot through a window
doing her a favor she didn't take a liking to

All was forgiven when
after a ginned-up group picture
they tore into a roast chicken

LAMENT WITH A FEW LINES IN NEW YORK

I picture the lungs as an accordion
that opens into a city.
So as not to wake your neighbors,

you play it quietly in bed.
Honeybees fill a tamarisk.
A hummingbird nests in a flaming tree

on a spider's web and a few blond hairs
blown when my wife snipped off her braid.
By the way, she still looks pretty,

although the world has broken her
days into worry beads. Nothing helps.
Not the hummingbird babies to be born

blind, with no feathers or father.
Nor the bee that leaves this sphere
stinging me, as my dearest, a Capricorn,

injects a tincture of doom.
She can take my breath away.
Or push the air out of a room,

like so much you and I cannot recall
or alter. But that is us
at the candy store for sure.

In a city with kids outside
alone, early or late.
Freedom was something

we understood as food.
Both taken for granted.
I can still hear the fruit seller's

Watermelon! a cry
of victory over politicians
and executioners.

Eventually they win.
But listen carefully
while he lugs his heavy pushcart up our street.

Fresh! Sweet!
Inconsolable.
An old incantation of humanity.

It fills the lungs. And mind
like a floating cloud.
The pigeons still coo,

clinging to the roof rail.
All the coughing on the planet
obscures tonight's bright star.

May it not yet be our sign to quit.
Better kin than us
were not so lucky.

To cross the desert
must have seemed impossible.
After seasons of plagues

I always wonder why God
led our people roundabout out of Egypt.
Forty years! Every day an eternity.

I missed the whole story
about how many perished in the sand.
While you sweated Hebrew school

I bicycled around the island.
Somehow I managed to place myself
in a desert. As far

as my wife and I are concerned,
clouds gather but no rain.
Don't know what else to say,

although we are saved to testify,
as a lifeless pin oak blooms
yellow out your fifth-floor window

the winter we've been calling,
regaling all the buried
from our childhood with a warm spring

again. Except for a poor crown
of hair, our *zayde*'s head glistens
as when his wife shined

the wrong car. In a year he's gone
from broke to working class
to burial, collapsing over toast.

Now the Millers overspill their row,
the loam pasty in graveyard light.
No one to console them.

No one allowed out.
The news is bad, blown nest,
eggs of broken blood vessels.

Our voices snag on yucca spikes,
two sentries asking why
has the next moment not arrived?

As if the world were once made
for a young king and queen
but the waters have risen over their heads.

THE QUEEN LOVES ROSES, THE PEASANT LOVES ROSES AND SHADE

To make if earthly possible more night
Roman emperors stab out the eyes

for ortolans to gorge in the perpetual dark
in cages carpeted with millet and fresh figs

each two ounces of mistaken fate
no sooner fattened up

drown and marinate in hot Armagnac
before roasting quickly

the vassals of the sovereign drape towels over their heads
to cage the scent and hide their shame from God

the guests commence to chew through minuscule rib cages
delicate as threads you might thrum on a tiny cello

because you would not shoot the little songbird out of the sky
without destroying it rendering it inedible

certain poachers smear glue
so the ortolans adhere to vines and branches

rather than continue on a path to Africa
life alters persuasively as I cross seventy

being a careerist neither songbird nor emperor
desire passes in and out

the oracle gives one answer only
youthful folly

the great dramas of history wheel
and crush one's feet after the offer

of a lifetime as an infinitesimal nebula
of the universe the spirit simply

builds a nest of cinnamon twigs and ignites it
to make if earthly possible more night

STAND IN THE RAIN OR NOT. NEVER TO
SPLASH IN A FOUNTAIN OR SWIM IN A SEA

Driving supplies to French hospitals
clouds rushing across the lenses
of your wire-armed glasses
in your Ford open-topped two-seater
Gertrude you had a fascist protector
that fact should not be
parsed and erased as the wind
herded the clouds over a nearby village
another puce-faced Gestapo
bastard of a flea crushed
on a bedsheet in an orphanage
dragged forty-four children
from their plates of apples
and lunchmeat to their death

Trying to remove it from the frame
Alice stamps her foot
on the portrait of Madame Cézanne
to roll it to save it to sell
art as collateral in what the fuck world
is the excrement of the innocent
not as valuable
the mind shatters to think
of the bones disfigured
in their shroud coats
stamped and numbered
and if possible still human
as the polished boot of a Nazi
presses a child's neck

POETRY OPPOSED TO RELIGION

She crushes the grapes herself with clean feet
while she sips brandy and eats chestnuts
or so the story goes the mash feels like pearly come
she'd rather trust a late pink hollyhock
blooming in a horse's ear than a portent
hurrying through the heavy green shadows
when the barn and the other houses burn
that's not enough siege no
she can't get back in so the smoke proceeds to
finish her rescue dogs in a hellstorm
of hot wind she understands that
in the ancient lyric there's a contemporary narrative
about disaster and death it's a brutal business
clearing the char she's got a ruthless grip
she owns that and the nightgown she ran out in

WHAT CAN RUN BUT NEVER WALKS, HAS A MOUTH BUT NEVER TALKS, HAS A HEAD BUT NEVER WEEPS, HAS A BED BUT NEVER SLEEPS? A RIVER. A SONNET

Hands soft and empty and free of intention
you're pressing the new wine even though you're dead
you have taken to stacking roof tiles as books you'll never read
I've learned from strangers you may be living
in a mountain temple a splash of light
do you remember we drifted on a lake
with your head in my lap so you could say I am unhappy
the dark lowers its voice the candles light themselves
suspended like the bones of the spine
boys in the chorus with the highest voices
must perform because Schubert cannot
he is sitting in the middle of a field of unrequited love
he has your hands
you finish dressing finally one fake earring then the other

CONSOLATION AND MISERY

An adolescent in a black wetsuit
with her ponytail pulled tight

pops up on a pink surfboard
the wind tosses around

midafternoon
the beach disappears in the tide

she rides the darkling sky
inside the cresting wave

lifts into air
once reserved for royalty

she was as sacred as a cave
it is forbidden to go in

wearing her sheath
she falls asleep in a fresh bed

awakens
as a pelican on the ocean

with its great wingspan
the board slaps her

it seems nonchalantly
the sunset fills the sea

with nightfall
black as the presence of all

color in art
in life is the absence

she swims for
the trapdoor

her heart pounds
to get out

drowns
thinking up is down

beauty sees its mistake
too late

while others cleaned fish
prepared them and went home

OYSTERS IN WEST MARIN

Fog softens the ringing
triangles of masts at the marina

your caller bicycles through
the air slow as a sail

lightly jingling her bell
to rendezvous with you

at a restaurant boasting
local oysters require no feed

no fertilizer or cultivation
live on a few acres of inlet bottom

nerves taut face soft
sitting hurts your joints

you order a shucked plate
the musk of rock pool at low tide

along this curve of marsh
umbrella pines obscure the bay

quiet until stormy Adrienne
braced for inquiry on a stage

you tilt the craggy shell
sip the liquor

to coax the soft meat
kiss the sea on the lips

when we meet again
your spirit steals by

for the last tepid wine
still as slack water

before a great ship
sails on for profit

an egret flies through the moonlight

DINNER PARTY

When the feast approaches
on a sylvan scene of lilacs and lovebirds
painted on ceramic, it's given to me
to serve, just as fate sometimes
intrudes on the marauder
to travel the seven seas
sporting a silver yacht,
sleeping on softened linen sheets.
The test could just as easily involve me
neglecting to open a door for somebody.
What does that say without a single word?
It says ordinary unqualified grief awaits.

PABLO CASALS, SAND DOLLAR
WITH EMBOSSED DRAWING

Maestro you exist as a shadow
of sorrowful countrymen

at the mercy of turbulent current
afloat a cello

holding fast
under the bridge of a Bach suite

drawing the bow across an abyss
you're intent on it and we listen

as children with a gate flung open
go out early on a walk for a lark

tyrants put tanks in the street
prehistoric creatures with guns mounted on their heads

wedged between the Mediterranean and the coast
Pablo pulls the sea across his body

his body across the sea
he must use his beauty

because his hands are busy
someone is pulling threads out of God

others cut the threads
and go to war over them O the sadness

of the impress of a dead hand in the sand

PILGRIMS VERSUS EMPERORS

For what is at stake on this day in history
the Emperor of France abdicated his throne

his invasion of Russia having imploded
he spent a first exile on the scented isle of Elba

building roads draining marshes raising cows and mules
and eventually a navy for his escape

after a bloody Waterloo is banished farther
to the southern Atlantic absorbing himself

with the meaning of life by all accounts
defeated one more time by poison or cancer

wealth honor and power weren't enough
Napoleon invited a mistress for many happy hours

eating cherries with her and lazing under a cypress
in his hubris he thought he could teach

religion to popes and science to scientists
clearly one's fantasies

like one's collected poems amount to far less
than six months of butterflies

in the souls of ancient relatives
in an elegant irony on Earth

we call them monarchs
proud pilgrims returned to a badland

after a far journey from winter
the migrants deserve to rest in a fine torpor

gazing inward into mystery again
because of heat and fire

they can barely share the pecan forest
once in a sea of emerald plants now spare

with the sugary liquid called honeydew that they adore
the visitors huddle together for shelter

enduring the high-pitched whistle
from the nearby prison at Yuma

they wear yellow and black stripes
under a scant canopy of leaves and green nut husks

as when they hid in the nectar
of the milkweed flower

in their natural system
of desire and truth

the truth would be death
walking around do we even notice

if the few trees have leaves or needles
if the visitors changed into dreams

is it too late to protect them
empty of rain maybe it feels

no worse outside time
last droplets asleep behind draped eyelids

on a warm October morning
the golden angle of sun along the horizon

sets a crown upon your life

FORAGER

Time comes to open the door
a spaniel bred to flush game
trails you slipping
along the bank
the fog only partially lifted

I begin to hear voices

too near the river
you stoop for rocks
the limestone mottled
your head feels like an animal
dead in the wall

you weight your coat
you wear the royal robe reluctantly
bombed from your house twice
your brain hurts like it's teething
your circle hoped you were discovered

in a barn or village shop
Virginia without your stick
your footprints and your hat
loosed to the cold
around noon on a Friday

I begin to hear voices

once you had written
about things people don't tell
silence chose for you
to step into a pebbly bed
as a bee sent to gather water

that follows other orders

THE BELL SLURS IN THE BLOWING SPRAY

Fan Bing throws herself
over a river's bridge
over a boy

Successful Marcel
& hobbled Najima
choke from influenza

Gone soon
skinny Gregor
drives too fast

Lucia the doctor
scorches on Mars
& you reader

it requires
all your humility
not to remark

glad it wasn't me
on the way out
everybody thinks that

the bell slurs
in the blowing spray
on a burning lake

on a day off
far from land
you hear a downpour

flog a tin roof
hear hot oil
pop peppers

hosing feces & eating
from stale tins
gets pretty insulting

but once adrift work is work

HEAVEN RUSHING OUT

The story begins with philosophy and ends with desire
using Wittgenstein's leaky boat
that one must repair while at sea
I row with no radio no bucket
around the next quickening bend
beauty appears unbound
the great berg shears into black ocean
as a glacial coliseum and I its tourist
is there a word for facing it
as I looked when I first saw you
in sheer clothing and me in dry ice
completely rearranged inside
saying take me slowly and then suddenly
a finger stirs the arctic floe
as if in the pool of my cocktail
fresh melt meets warming water
confounding themselves my mistake as well
toppling like a drunk overboard
to the rest of the world merely
cut as a word from a stanza
the detail blurs from here it seems
my darling paces on the shore
in a soft shawl and a hard shell
of reality in the worst sort of breakup poem
with no rhyme or reason
our end resists the love of our lives
the only thing harder than leaving first

stiff as a wall of mineral cliff

is the mineral cold knowledge of the survivor

trying to herd ice as it melts

like thoughts once gathered into facts

the world is everyone who is still here

ice fishing and burning sage at sea

scrambling for berries and seeds on farms

the hoarding of walnuts frenzies the throng

one faithful page hurrying in the wind

carries a violin like a burnt wing

ACKNOWLEDGMENTS

To be able to publish books of poetry with the same publishing house over most of a lifetime is an incomparable gift from Michael Wiegers and the Copper Canyon Press group. Thank you!

Many thanks to the editors of the following magazines, journals, and online publications in which some of these poems first appeared, especially to Cal Bedient, firebrand and friend:

Boston Review, DIAGRAM, Girl Blood Info, Lana Turner: A Journal of Poetry and Opinion, The Missouri Review, The Volta, Written Here: The Community of Writers Poetry Review.

"The Lovers" is to the memory of Li Qingzhao, Song dynasty poet 1,000 years ago.

"Jade River" and "Bird with One Leg" are for Shangyang Fang.

"The Thatched Cottage" is for Jorie Graham, with opening lines improvised from "Song: How My Thatch Roof Was Blown Away by Autumn Winds," *The Selected Poems of Du Fu,* translated by Burton Watson (Columbia University Press, 2002).

"Paper Banners" borrows the phrase "all is to be dared" from Fragment 31 in *If Not, Winter: Fragments of Sappho,* translated by Anne Carson (Alfred A. Knopf, 2002).

"Lament with a Few Lines in New York" is for Caryn Miller.

"Stand in the Rain or Not. Never to Splash in a Fountain or Swim in a Sea" is in memory of Gertrude Stein and Alice B. Toklas.

"Poetry Opposed to Religion" and "What Can Run but Never Walks, . . ." are elegies for Jane Mead.

"Oysters in West Marin" is in memory of Adrienne Rich.

"Pablo Casals, Sand Dollar with Embossed Drawing" is in memory of the cellist and humanitarian.

"Forager" is in memory of Virginia Woolf.

"Heaven Rushing Out" is the name of acupuncture point Conception Vessel 22.

ABOUT THE AUTHOR

Jane Miller is the author of twelve books of poems and two col-
lections of essays on poetry. She taught poetry workshops and
seminars for many years as a professor at the University of Arizona
and served as a visiting poet at many other programs, including the
Iowa Writers' Workshop and the Michener Center for Writers in
Austin, Texas. She lives in Tucson, Arizona.

Poetry is vital to language and living. Since 1972, Copper Canyon Press has published extraordinary poetry from around the world to engage the imaginations and intellects of readers, writers, booksellers, librarians, teachers, students, and donors.

WE ARE GRATEFUL FOR THE MAJOR SUPPORT PROVIDED BY:

academy of american poets

THE PAUL G. ALLEN
FAMILY FOUNDATION

amazon literary partnership

POETRY FOUNDATION

4
CULTURE

Lannan

the point
envision·enact·evolve

National Endowment for the Arts
arts.gov
ART WORKS.

WASHINGTON STATE
ARTS COMMISSION

A&
OFFICE OF ARTS & CULTURE
SEATTLE

The Witter Bynner Foundation
for Poetry

TO LEARN MORE ABOUT UNDERWRITING
COPPER CANYON PRESS TITLES,
PLEASE CALL 360-385-4925 EXT. 103

WE ARE GRATEFUL FOR THE MAJOR SUPPORT PROVIDED BY:

Richard Andrews and
  Colleen Chartier
Anonymous
Jill Baker and Jeffrey Bishop
Anne and Geoffrey Barker
Donna Bellew
Will Blythe
John Branch
Diana Broze
John R. Cahill
Sarah Cavanaugh
Keith Cowan and Linda Walsh
Stephanie Ellis-Smith and
  Douglas Smith
Mimi Gardner Gates
Gull Industries Inc.
  on behalf of William True
William R. Hearst III
Carolyn and Robert Hedin
David and Jane Hibbard
Bruce S. Kahn
Phil Kovacevich and Eric Wechsler

Lakeside Industries Inc.
  on behalf of Jeanne Marie Lee
Maureen Lee and Mark Busto
Ellie Mathews and Carl Youngmann
  as The North Press
Larry Mawby and Lois Bahle
Hank and Liesel Meijer
Petunia Charitable Fund and
  adviser Elizabeth Hebert
Madelyn S. Pitts
Suzanne Rapp and Mark Hamilton
Adam and Lynn Rauch
Emily and Dan Raymond
Joseph C. Roberts
Cynthia Sears
Kim and Jeff Seely
D.D. Wigley
Barbara and Charles Wright
In honor of C.D. Wright,
  from Forrest Gander
Caleb Young as C. Young Creative
The dedicated interns and faithful
  volunteers of Copper Canyon Press

The pressmark for Copper Canyon Press suggests
entrance, connection, and interaction
while holding at its center
an attentive, dynamic space for poetry.

This book is set in Optima Nova LT Pro.
Book design by Gopa & Ted2, Inc.

Printed in the USA
CPSIA information can be obtained
at www.ICGtesting.com
JSHW021420290424
62133JS00003B/88

9 781556 596735